How to Respond to . . .
THE LODGE

How to Respond to . . .

THE LODGE

L. James Rongstad

Publishing House
St. Louis

THE RESPONSE SERIES

Concordia Publishing House, St. Louis, Missouri
Copyright © 1977 Concordia Publishing House
Manufactured in the United States of America

Library of Congress Cataloging in Publication Data

Rongstad, James.
        How to respond to . . . the Lodge.

        (Response series)
        1. Freemasons. I. Title.
HS395.R66   366′.1   77-10043
ISBN 0-570-07677-3

Forword to the Response Series

This series of booklets serves as a response to the need expressed by the members of The Lutheran Church—Missouri Synod assembled in national convention at Anaheim, Calif., July 1975, for specialized literature to assist in the "evangelization of persons who belong to anti-Christian sects and cults."

Those who were responsible for responding to that need, which the convention put into a formal resolution, called on others to explore the need further. The result was the development of this series of booklets. It was felt that the need was best summed up by St. Peter when he advised Christians "always be ready to answer anyone who asks you to explain the hope you have, but be gentle and respectful" (1 Peter 3:15 Beck).

In today's society, where cults, sects, and movements have multiplied, it is often difficult for the Christian to feel confident that he is "ready to answer." This series is planned to help the Christian in that dilemma by providing him information about cults by comparing the teachings of cults with the Christian faith.

Some of the cults are very evangelistic, seeking to make converts of everyone who will listen. This series also seeks to help the Christian share his faith with those who seek to evangelize him, and to do so in a "gentle and respectful" way, as Peter suggests. For that reason each of the books not only seeks to compare the basic teachings of the cult with Christianity but suggests how to witness to its members.

The booklets are intended to be used in two ways. They can be read and studied by an individual who is confronted with a specific need to know about one cult, or they can be studied in a series by a Bible study group. The series is introduced by the "foundation" book, which provides an overview of "cult mentality" and the more general problems posed by cults in our culture. The series continues with selecting some of the larger or more influential groups for coverage in a specific booklet.

The series begins with the foundation booklet and five specific ones. It is hoped that, after the successful acceptance of this first issue by the church, other specific booklets can be added, dealing with those cults that are for the moment of most concern to Christian people.

> Erwin J. Kolb, *Executive Secretary*
> The Board for Evangelism
> The Lutheran Church—Missouri Synod

Editor's Preface

Rev. L. James Rongstad is a native of Minnesota, now residing in Louisiana.

Upon completion of high school, Pastor Rongstad spent five years in the United States Navy before entering Concordia Theological Seminary, Springfield, Ill., from which he graduated in 1958.

Pastor Rongstad has had wide experience in pastoral counseling, particularly in the area of problems faced by young people today. His interest in the spiritual implications of membership in a religious lodge grew out of his concern that Christian people maintain an undivided witness to the one and only Gospel of Jesus Christ. Pastor Rongstad, in this little book, delineates the incompatibilities between religious universalism as it is exemplified in the lodges and that explicit Christian confession and testimony that is enjoined upon all Christians by the Savior's own words, "Whosoever therefore shall confess Me before men, him will I confess also before My Father which is in heaven. But whosoever shall deny Me before men, him will I also deny before My Father which is in heaven" (Matt. 10:32-33 KJV).

In resolving the contradictions between lodge theology and the Bible's explicit doctrines, Pastor Rongstad urges serious study of the theological positions of both the lodge and the church.

Philip Lochhaas, *Executive Secretary*
The Commission on Organizations
The Lutheran Church—Missouri Synod

Contents

Introduction

Soren Kierkegaard said, "Christendom has done away with Christianity without being quite aware of it." Many 20th-century Christians are, and have been, giving away their heritage to the philosophies of liberalty, tolerance, and compromise. Moral values, the basis for establishing life-styles, are being established by public opinion rather than God's Word. It seems that our declining self-discipline and our rising self-indulgence can be compared to sinking ground and shifting sand. The very foundation on which our principles were founded has nearly disappeared. Someone has "pulled the rug out from under us." That "rug" is the authority of the Bible to determine our moral values, our life principles, goals and priorities, yes, our very salvation.

The time has come for us to "blow the whistle" in order to stop our mad rush into oblivion. We need to reflect, using the Holy Scripture. The standard of God's Word will reveal the philosophies and systems which are "knocking the props out from under us." Fingers need to be pointed. Change must come, only this time the change must be back to the Bible.

This volume is part of a small effort to create some changes. It is one of several booklets which will help you have factual information on which to base opinions and make judgments. It is written in order to preserve among us our priceless heritage of a people saved by God's grace through faith in Jesus Christ, true God and true man, the Savior of the world. We pray that you will be always prepared to give every man an account of the hope that is in you. May you be READY TO GIVE AN ANSWER TO THE LODGE.

1
History of the Lodge

Organizationally lodgery began with modern Freemasonry in 1717 A. D. Two clergymen, Dr. James Anderson, a Presbyterian, and Dr. John Theophilus Desaguliers, a French Hugenot turned Anglican, stimulated others to form a select group. This inspired four London speculative lodges to come together and form the first Grand Lodge.

This historical fact, however, does not stop the *Ancient, Free, and Accepted Masons* (A. F. & A. M.) from teaching prospective members that their origin is traceable to King Solomon. They say that Hiram, King of Tyre, aided in the building of the Jerusalem Temple by supplying trees, carpenters, and masons for this project, and that he had close relations with the great King Solomon concerning problems of mutual interest. This relationship, it is claimed by the *New Age,* official organ of the Supreme Council Southern Jurisdiction (April, 1961, p. 30), " . . . tends to confirm the belief that there was some close Masonic tie between them."

The Holy Bible—Masonic Edition, published by John A. Hertel Co., says of the probable antiquity of the lodge, "It is admitted that Masonry is descended from the ancient mysteries. These were first arranged when the constellation Leo was at the summer solstice. Thus the antiquity of Masonry was written in the starry heavens" (Revised Edition, 1957, p. 21).

Albert Pike in *Morals and Dogma* (p. 277), says, "The first Masonic legislator whose memory is preserved to us by history was Buddha, who, about a thousand years before the Christian era, reformed the religion of Manous. He called to the priesthood all men, without distinction of caste, who felt themselves inspired by God to instruct men."

On May 17, 1963, the *Birmingham News* (Ala.), in a special edition dedicated to the Masonic Order, reprinted a statement made by T. G. Brabston, the late distinguished leader of the Southeastern Shrine Association, "The origin of Freemasonry is lost in the nebulous mist of unrecorded history. It has been identified with the building of King Solomon's temple. The reliable history of Masonry covers the past 250 years."

Because of the word "lodge" some would have us believe that its use in 1278 to refer to a hut or shed for shelter at the site of a new building was really a "lodge" in the sense of an organization like we have today. Such temporary buildings housed tools, were workshops, offices, and sleeping quarters for the workmen, some of whom were masons, while they were away from their homes. These ancient "lodges" would compare with the oil rigs in the Gulf of Mexico of today, because these perched dwellings become the temporary homes of the men at work.

Occasionally a mason may be heard to claim that John the Baptizer, the evangelist John, Noah, and the people at the Tower of Babel were all fellow masons. But these claims cannot be substantiated. They are at best the fruits of fertile imaginations and pride in the order. In the absence of documentary evidence to link Freemasonry to any time prior to 1717 A. D., those who claim a lengthy antiquity simply ignore the facts. The more reliable, honest, and respected Masonic leaders of today are not anxious to support a lengthy history. Many freely admit the truth.

In spite of the dispute with respect to the organizational antiquity of Freemasonry, the time period of its existence has had a great influence on the world. It is the "Granddaddy" of all lodges. Its teachings, rituals, customs, and practices, and its secrecy have had an inspirational effect on other similar groups such as the Moose, Eagles, Elks, and the National Grange. All of them, by comparison, seem to be patterned after the Masonic Lodge.

Great American men have been Masons. Hertel's *Holy Bible—Masonic Edition* claims 15 presidents have been Masons: Washington, Jefferson, Madison, Monroe, Jackson, Polk, Buchanan, Johnson, Garfield, McKinley, T. Roosevelt, Taft, Harding, F. D. Roosevelt, and Truman. Some think Pierce and Taylor were also in that number. Furthermore, it is claimed that Lincoln and Grant had proposed to become Masons, but death came to both of them before they took the vows. The American name most cherished by Masons is that of George Washington, to whom is built a huge monument on a commanding hill in view of the Potomac River in Arlington, Va. It is simply magnificent!

Even as Masons have influenced American politics and history, so also has Masonry influenced American religious life. In 1769 the first Knights Templar degrees were conferred by the lodge. This group of Christians was assumed into Freemasonry, being made a part of the York Rite, in order to make the lodge more acceptable to professing Christians. The Knights Templar are inspired by the Crusaders of medieval times and are supposed to be militant supporters of Christianity. Conscientious Christians often think that the Knights Templar Degree is not objectionable, and even point with pride to their Order. They tend to forget, however, that by their association with the lodge they also support the teachings of the whole. Admittedly the lodge had a Christian orientation, and still uses much of the Bible's teachings, but as it evolved it developed the concept of Deism—a non-specific belief about who God is, a generalized view of Deity. This has confused many Christians. If the Triune God of the Christians could be understood as just one of the gods men worship, then none would be offended, all could become a part of the lodge. The Masonic Grand Master in England, the Duke of Sussex, in 1913, gave rise to "universalism" when he influenced the English lodge to omit Christ's name from their prayers. Today the influence of the lodge can be seen especially in the Unitarian—Universalist Church and The Church of Jesus Christ in the Latter Day Saints (Mormons). Many church buildings of various denominations have cornerstones displaying the lodge symbols. Lodges have been welcomed by various denominations to participate in the conducting of funerals.

2
Understanding Lodge Concepts

Although discussion of religion and politics is strictly forbidden in the lodge, it is necessary to establish whether or not Masonry is a religion. Authoritative Masonic sources do not help us to arrive at an answer because quotations can be found in Masonic literature which both claim and disclaim that Masonry is a religion. The avoidance of religious discussion does not mean that the lodge is not a religion. All it means is that the members may not talk about their individual denominations, their individual religions—as they avoid political talk. Such talk would create tensions and disagreements.

What is religion? A dictionary definition say: (1) The service and adoration of God or a God as expressed in forms of worship. (2) One of the systems of faith and worship. (3) The profession or practice of religious beliefs; religious observances collectively; pl., rites. (4) Devotion of fidelity; conscientiousness. (5) An awareness or conviction of the existence of a supreme being, arousing reverence, love, gratitude, the will to obey and serve, and the like; as, man only is capable of religion. Does this apply to Freemasonry?

Freemasonry is a system of morality developed and inculcated by the science of symbolism. Veiled in allegory, lodge teachings are taught by the use of symbols. The all-seeing eye reminds one of God. The first question asked of the candidate as he enters the Entered Apprentice Degree, the first step of the three-step "Blue Lodge," is if he believes in God. The lodge is not interested in hearing who the candidate thinks God is, rather, they prohibit an atheist from joining the lodge. The name used by the Mason in reference to God is "Supreme Architect of the Universe," or "Supreme Grand Master," or "The Nameless One of a Hundred Names."

After an impressive ceremony, the Entered Apprentice is presented with the lambskin apron because the lamb has in all ages been deemed an emblem of innocence. "He therefore who wears the Lambskin, or White Leather Apron as the badge of a Mason, is thereby continually reminded of that purity of conduct in life which is so essentially necessary to his gaining admission to the celestial lodge where the Supreme Architect of the Universe presides." This man-centered theology, emphasizing the ultimate reward of heaven to the faithful Mason, eliminates the necessity for the redeeming work of Jesus. The Bible teaches that we are saved by grace alone. Works follow our justification, demonstrating our obedience to our Lord Jesus Christ because of His Gift of salvation given to us.

In every Masonic lodge there are three indispensable pieces of furniture. They are the Square, the Compass, and the Sacred Book. The Sacred Book is controversial. In a lodge made up primarily of Christians, the Holy Bible is used. The Pentateuch of the Jews and the Koran of the Mohammedan are also considered Sacred Books in Freemasonry. So also are any other "Sacred Books" of other religions. The lodge does not want to offend anyone. Rather it sees itself as above all religions in the world. Pike, in *Morals and Dogma*, says, "Perfect truth is not attainable anywhere . . . it

11

is our duty always to press forward in the search; for though absolute truth is unattainable, yet the amount of error in our views is capable of progressive and perpetual diminution; and thus Masonry is a continual struggle toward the light." This attitude of condescension toward specific religions is really an elevation of the lodge as a super-religion.

The Square and Compass are basic tools of the builder. As they are used to make things square or round, so also the Mason is reminded that symbolically he, too, must continue the individual self-analysis to insure that he is living a morally upright life.

Ashlar is stone taken from the quarry. Rough and jagged, it is to remind the Mason of his imperfect nature. The gavel reminds him that as it removes the rough and jagged edges making the ashlar smooth, so also is he to remove imperfections in his personality and life-style.

All of this has religious or philosophical meaning for the Mason. It can be summed up by saying that Masonry teaches man that he is not originally sinful, just imperfect; that if he works faithfully at keeping the principles of Freemasonry he will be welcomed into the Grand Lodge Above where the Supreme Grand Master presides. This is universalism, deism, and humanism. This denies the necessity of having a Savior.

Coil's *Masonic Encyclopedia* (1961), in a lengthy article on "Religion" says,

> Some attempt to avoid the issue by saying that Freemasonry is not a religion but is religious, seeming to believe that the substitution of an adjective for a noun makes a fundamental difference. It would be as sensible to say that a man had no intellect but was intellectual or that he had no honor but was honorable. . . . Freemasonry certainly requires a belief in the existence of, and man's dependence upon, a Supreme Being to which he is responsible. What can a church add to that, except to bring into fellowship those who have like feelings? That is exactly what the lodge does. . . . It is said that Freemasonry is not sectarian, by which is meant that it has not identified itself with any well-known sect. But, if it has a religious credo, may it not, itself, constitute a sect to be added to the others? . . . Perhaps the most we can say is that Freemasonry has not generally been regarded as a sect or denomination, though it may become so if its religious practices, creeds, tenets, and dogma increase as much in the future as they have in the past. Only by judging from external appearances and applying arbitrary gauges can we say that Freemasonry is not religion. . . . Nothing herein is intended to be an argument that Freemasonry *ought* to be a religion; our purpose is simply to determine what it has *become* and *is*.

Greece, in January 1970, banned the Masonic lodge from the country, stating that it was, for them, an illegal, secret religion.

Secrecy so dominates the lodge that the candidate, *before* he knows what he is getting into, must take his oath under the most severe penalties. For instance, he must "always conceal and never reveal" the secrets of Masonry, and if he does he gives permission to "have my tongue torn out by the roots, my left breast torn open, my heart plucked out, my body severed in twain, my bowels taken from thence and burned to ashes and scattered to the four winds of heaven."

A paradox exists. Masonry is in search of the Truth, yet the Mason must always conceal and never reveal Masonic teachings. The lodge will not confess that Jesus is the Truth (John 14:6). Pike, in *Morals and Dogma,* p. 161, says:

> But Masonry teaches, and has preserved in their purity, the cardinal tenets of the old primitive faith, which underlie and are the foundation of all religions. All that ever existed have had a basis of truth; and all have overlaid that truth with errors. The primitive truths taught by the Redeemer were sooner corrupted, and intermingled and alloyed with fictions than when taught to the first of our race. Masonry is the universal morality which is suitable to the inhabitants of every clime, to the man of every creed.

Evaluate whether the following two quotations from non-Masonic orders merely recognize that God exists or whether they go farther to the establishment of religion: "There is no death; life is full of mysteries until the God of Love opens the portals of His kingdom and bids each passing soul a glorious welcome into its eternal home. . . . Let us bow our heads in silent prayer for our sisters who are waiting in the Great Auxiliary over there" (from the Charter Draping Ceremony, Auxiliary to the Fraternal Order of Eagles). "Surely there is an after-life for all who have been loyal and true, a life to which light and peace shall come, where the burden shall be lifted and the heartache shall cease, where the love, the hope, and the fulfillment that escapes us here shall be given to us to be ours forever" (Funeral Service, American Legion Auxiliary).

The foregoing is adequate to show how the teachings of Christianity are lumped together in the stew pot of all religions. The uniqueness of the Christian message, grounded in the hope of eternal life secured for us by the Resurrection of Jesus from the dead, is threatened by organizations who reduce salvation to mere moral living without the emphasis on sin and grace, repentance and forgiveness in Christ.

The Mason, when confronted with the contradictions in the teachings of lodgery and Christianity, ususally retreats into his shell of secrecy. In-depth discussion is avoided. Quite possibly he thinks of himself as above sectarian differences and so refuses with politeness to openly talk. Committed Christians, however, are always eager to "make a defense to anyone who calls you to account for the hope that is in you." We want you, dear reader, to also be READY TO GIVE AN ANSWER TO THE LODGE.

3

Organization and Structure of the Lodge

Freemasonry, dating from 1717 A. D., is represented in the United States by the Blue Lodge of three basic degrees: Entered Apprentice, Fellow Craft, and Master Mason.

Beyond the Blue Lodge, the Master Mason may choose one of two paths to follow—or he may choose neither. The two paths are Scottish Rite and American Rite (sometimes called York Rite). The Scottish Rite has 30 degrees beyond the Blue Lodge, the last of which is the 33d degree, a strictly honorary award. There are 10 degrees beyond the Blue Lodge in the York Rite, culminating in the Knights Templar Degree, the equivalent of the 32d degree in the Scottish Rite. The first three degrees of the Blue Lodge are the only essential degrees through which all Masons must pass. All other degrees are optional.

Some side Orders in Masonry are the Tall Cedars in Lebanon of the United States of America, the Mystic Order of Veiled Prophets of the Enchanted Realm (Grotto), Knights of the Red Cross of Constantine, and Acacia Fraternity.

Affiliated female organizations include the Order of the Eastern Star, White Shrine of Jerusalem, Order of Amaranth, Daughters of the Nile, and Daughters of Mokanna.

Youth organizations are Order of the Builders, Order of DeMolay, Order of Job's Daughters, and Order of the Rainbow.

The first Grand Lodge was formed in London, England, in 1717 A. D., when four local lodges came together. From this Grand Lodge, all the other Grand Lodges in the world, 104 of them, have been authorized. In the United States there are 49 Grand Lodges.

The lodge, be it local or regional, is not democratically governed. Rather, rule is autocratic. The Worshipful Master of a local lodge, for example, has supreme and total control. The by-laws of the local lodge do set minimum standards of conduct, but usually are so worded as to place all authority in the hands of the elected leader.

The expression "Blue Lodge" comes from two theories. One is that when "operative masons" (medieval craft workers) considered the blue sky to be symbolic of the purity of God they should be reminded to work harder to keep pure their own lives. The other theory is that shortly after "speculative Masonry" (symbolic Masonry, begun in 1717 A. D.) came into existence, the color blue was substituted for white as the official color for the first Grand Lodge of England, presumably because blue was the color of the Order of the Garter of which a number of Masonic leaders were members.

It appears that most lodges, especially the Masonic Lodge, discriminate racially (even as they freely admit "unanimous consent" is necessary for any candidate to be "entered" into the craft). Negro Freemasonry started in the United States on March 6, 1775, in Boston, when the degrees of Masonry were conferred upon Prince Hall and 14 other Black men in a military lodge (No. 441 on the Irish Register) in the English

Army attached to the 38th Regiment. It is alleged that Prince Hall was born in Barbadoes, British West Indies, that he came to Boston and became leader of "free" negroes of that city, and was ordained a minister. On Sept. 29, 1784 the Grand Lodge of England issued a charter for African Lodge No. 459 of Boston. It was instrumental in forming the first Negro Grand Lodge in the United States.

The term "Freemason," according to Masonic sources, predates the organizational origins of the lodge. A number of explanations are suggested, such as: (1) Masons worked in free stone—which could be carved—and hence were called "free-stone masons," later shortened to "freemasons." (2) They were free men, not serfs. (3) They were free to move from place to place as they might desire. (4) They were given the freedom of the towns or localities in which they worked. (5) They were free of the rules and regulations that were usually imposed upon members of guilds. These "freemasons" are referred to being "operative" because they worked at their specific trades, such as builders, stone masons, architects, designers engaged in constructive work. Because they usually worked closely together, and because they frequently were away from home, they formed a tight-knit group in which they shared discussions on philosophies, politics, religion, and all other interests of their society.

Gradually these "operatives" were joined by others who were not of their crafts, but because they were interested in the background and teachings of the operative fraternity, they were considered to be "accepted" or "speculative" masons. Now all members are accepted as "speculative masons." That is why the name, "Ancient, Free, and Accepted Masons."

The York or American Rite Masonry has 10 degrees beyond the Blue Lodge, divided into three categories. Degrees 4—7 comprise the "Chapter." They are the "Capitular Degrees." Numerically ordered, they are called Mark Master, Past Master, Most Excellent Master, and Royal Arch Mason. The second grouping is called the "Council," comprised of degrees 8, 9, and 10. These are called Royal Master, Select Master, and Super Excellent Master. The third grouping is called the "Commandery" and is comprised of the Order of Red Cross, Order of Knights of Malta, and finally Order of Knights Templar, the highest degree.

The degree structure of Scottish Rite Masonry is built around four groupings. The Lodge of Perfection has 11 degrees (4—14), commonly called the "Ineffable Degrees." The Council of Princes of Jerusalem has two degrees (15—16), called the "Historical Grades." The Chapter of Rose Croix has two degrees (17—18), called the "Philosophical Grades." The Consistory has the last 14 degrees (19—32), called the "Traditional and Chivalric Grades." The Thirty-Third (33d) Degree is the "Official Grade," strictly honorary. The cost of attaining the 32d degree after becoming a Master Mason lies somewhere between $100 and $150.

4

Salvation in the Lodge

There are three basic teachings of lodgery which must be taken as a whole to understand the concept of salvation. All lodges, be they Masonic, affiliates of Freemasony, the "animal lodges," etc., teach "the Fatherhood of God, the Brotherhood of Man, and the Immortality of the Soul." Our study has centered in the Masonic Order, and our following quotations are taken from their sources. However, the same basic teachings are found in other lodge fraternities as well.

The *Iowa Quarterly Bulletin* of April 1917, p. 54, says, "Masonry is a Divinely appointed institution, designed to draw men nearer to God, to give them a clearer conception of their proper relationship to God as their Heavenly Father, to men as their brethren and the ultimate destiny of the human soul." Let us take each of the three subjects separately for further study. The first is God. The second is man. The third is immortality of the human soul.

We assume our readers understand that the Christian and Biblical God is the Holy Trinity, three Persons yet one God, Father, Son, and Holy Spirit. Also that Jesus Christ is True God and True Man, that He is both divine and human, that as the Word He became Flesh in point of time; that He died to pay for our sins, was raised from the dead, and ascended into heaven, where He today lives and is aware of us.

Albert Pike, who has been called by fellow Masons "one of the most distinguished Masons the Western World has produced," says in *Morals and Dogmas,* p. 23 (this is also found in Hertel's *Bible,* p. 9):

> It (Masonry) reverences all the great reformers. It sees in Moses, the Law-giver of the Jews, in Confucius and Zoraster, in Jesus of Nazareth, and in the Arabian Iconoclast, Great Teachers of Morality, and Eminent Reformers, if no more; And allows every brother of the Order to assign to each such higher and even Divine Character as his Creed and Truth require. . . . We do not undervalue the importance of any Truth. We utter no word that can be deemed irreverent by anyone of any faith. We do not tell the Moslem that it is only important for him to believe that there is but one God, and wholly unessential whether Mahomet was His prophet. We do not tell the Hebrew that the Messiah whom he expects was born in Bethlehem nearly two thousand years ago; and that he is a heretic because he will not so believe. And as little do we tell the sincere Christian that Jesus of Nazareth was but a man like us, or His history but the unreal revival of an older legend. To do either is beyond our jurisdiction. Masonry, of no one age, belongs to all time; of on one religion, it finds its great truths in all. To every Mason, there is a God; One Supreme, Infinite in Goodness, Wisdom, Foresight, Justice, and Benevolence; Creator, Disposer, and Preserver of all things. How, or by what intermediates He creates and acts, and in what way He unfolds and manifests Himself, Masonry leaves to creeds and religions to inquire.

What kind of God is it that the Mason confesses? "G. A. O. T. U." "Great Architect of the Universe." This "confession," however, is a careful avoidance of any other "confessed" name found in the "creeds" and "religions."

The most secret word, assumed to be the word for God, is transmitted to the candidate as he is "raised" into the Master Mason Degree, as he assumes the position of the "five points of fellowship" (toe to toe, knee to knee, chest to chest, cheek to cheek, and mouth to ear). It is whispered: MAH—HA—BONE. This "sacred" word, the candidate is told, must never be spoken aloud, never revealed, and always concealed.

The Mason in the Royal Arch Degree (York Rite), a degree through which the Knight Templar is to pass on his way to the supposed "Christian Degree," has another secret name revealed to him at his initiation ceremony. The name of the True God, "re-discovered," is "Jah—Bul—On." This is the Royal Arch Masons' "Trinity." "Jah" is an abbreviation for the Hebrew name of God: JAHWEH, or JEHOVAH. "Bul" or "Bal" is the name for the Assyrian deity, and is mentioned throughout the Old Testament as "Baal" or "Baal-peor." (This is the idol God told the Israelites to avoid at all costs.) "On" is the Egyptian sun god.

In the Knights Templar Degree, where the emphasis is supposed to be on Jesus Christ, there is a strange absence of any reference to His being True God and True Man, divine and human. Beautiful language is used. Impressive adoration gives one the impression a Christian would expect. But what is not mentioned is Christ, the Savior from sin; nor repentance on the part of man. At this point it is now necessary to turn to the teaching about man.

The lodge teaching about the nature of man is altogether different from that of Christianity. As Christians, we confess the Scriptural truth that man is born in "the image of Adam," that is, sinful, corrupt, apart from God. Masonry never talks is these terms, nor that man is hopeless unless "saved" by a Redeemer. Ward, in *The Freemasonry: It's Aims and Ideals,* p. 187, says, "Freemasonry has taught each man can, by himself, work out his own conception of God and thereby achieve salvation." In effect, the Mason can determine his own god, and then the terms of his own salvation. It is a convenient arrangement. *The Short Talk Bulletin,* publication of the Masonic Service Association of the United States, Vol. 43, No. 5., May, 1964, p. 3, says, "The fraternity is, to me, man's organized attempt in an orderly way to proceed in a direction of life that is orientated toward what he feels is creation's design for him in this universe. It is the reach of man for God." Pike, in *Morals and Dogma,* p. 854f., says, "To achieve it (salvation) the Mason must first attain a solid conviction, founded upon reason, that he hath within him a spiritual nature, a soul that is not to die when the body is dissolved, but is to continue to exist and to advance toward perfection through all the ages of eternity, and to see more and more clearly, as it draws nearer unto God the light of the Divine Presence."

The third major teaching of the lodge is that of the immortality of the soul. Hertel's revised *Masonic Edition of the Bible* urges all Masons to be mindful of the symbolism of the various instruments by which man is to measure his life in order to determine his integrity for admission into the Grand Lodge above. It says, "Guided by the movable jewels of Masonry (the square, compass, level, and plumb), he builds for himself a character of unblamableness preparing himself as a successful candidate for admission in the Grand Lodge (p. 33)."

The *Louisiana Masonic Monitor,* p. 132, has the Worshipful Master reciting to the candidate for the Master Mason Degree these words:

> And now, my brethren, let us see to it, and so regulate our lives by the plumb-line of justice, ever squaring our actions by the square of virtue, that when the Grand Warden of Heaven shall call for us, we may be found ready.

To the candidate for the Entered Apprentice Degree this is said:

> You were presented a Lambskin or White Leather Apron. The Lamb has in all ages been deemed an emblem of innocence. By the Lambskin, therefore, the Mason is reminded of that purity of life and conduct which is essential to his gaining admission to the Celestial Lodge above, where the Supreme Architect of the Universe presides (*Monitor,* p. 44f.).

The Masonic doctrine of immortality is further illustrated in this prayer at the burial service of a fellow Mason:

> Most glorious God, Author of all good and Giver of all mercy, pour down Thy blessings upon us, and strengthen our solemn engagements with the ties of sincere affection. May the present instance of mortality remind us of our own approaching fate, and, by drawing our attention toward Thee, may we be induced so to regulate our conduct here than when the moment of dissolution shall arrive at which we must quit this brief scene, we may be received into Thine everlasting kingdom, there to enjoy that uninterrupted and unceasing felicity which is allotted to the souls of just men made perfect. Amen.
> Response—So mote it be (*Monitor,* p. 156f).

The lodge teaches, along with the immortality of the soul, a belief in the Resurrection of the body. Both ideas are seen in this statement at the burial service (which is spoken following the above quoted prayer):

> Quietly may thy body sleep in this earthly bed, my brother. Bright and glorious be thy rising from it. Fragant be the acacia (evergreen) sprig that here shall flourish. May the earliest buds of spring unfold their beauties on this, thy body's resting place; and here may the sweetness of the summer's rose linger latest. Though the cold blast of autumn may lay them in the dust, and for a time destroy the loveliness of their existence, yet their fading is not final, and in the springtime they shall surely bloom again. So in the bright morning of Resurrection thou shalt spring again into newness of life. Until then, dear brother, until then, farewell (*Monitor,* p. 157).

Need we point to the glaring absence of Jesus Christ? We are taught from the Holy Bible that there is no immortal life in heaven nor Resurrection of the glorified body apart from the victory of Jesus over death and our faith in Him, which is given to us by grace.

Evaluate the following from the Ritual of the Order of Amaranth: "Faith, as recorded by St. Paul, is the substance of things hoped for, the evidence of things not seen. . . . It upholds us in our darkest hours, and directs the mind to the contemplation of the goodness of our Divine Father, who doeth all things well, rewarding each according to his works.... Let us have faith in ourselves, in our associates, and struggle on against evil influences and discouragements; for by keeping Faith with one another we enhance the happiness of ourselves. Faith is the Savior and Redeemer of nations."

Another example of confused teaching with respect to God, man, and the immortality of the soul is this announcement from the Final Tribute to Deceased Members of the Fraternal Order of Eagles: "It is not a final parting. The Fraternal Order of Eagles teaches that we shall meet again, and that the tender associations of life are broken only to be reunited. Whether we look into the living eyes of those we love or gaze into the placid faces of our dead, love divine comforts us with the blessed assurance that this relation is eternal." Or consider this statement from the Loyal Order of Moose Burial service: "It is but a parting; a journey to an unknown shore; a journey which we, too, shall take—and at its end our Circle form again."

The Memorial Service of the Elks has this paragraph read by the Exalted Ruler:

As Elks we are taught that some day the mortal shall put on immortality. Firm in our faith, we are reminded by these services that we are born, not to die, but to live. True, the light of beloved eyes has faded from our sight, but it shines more brightly upon another shore. Voices we loved to hear at the fireside, in marts of trade, or in fraternal association, are silenced; but they will live again in the music of the Choir Invisible, and blend forever in the harmony of angels. Memorial Day with us is a day of tender sentiment. Hope dries our tears, and with eyes of faith we may see those whom we loved and lost awhile, faring on through a better land, awaiting the day when the chain of fraternal love shall be reunited forevermore.

5

Prayer and Syncretism in the Lodge

As mentioned earlier, the lodge thinks of itself as above religions. It seeks to offend none, yet adopts portions of the belief-systems of many. This is called "syncretism."

"Christianity taught the doctrine of Fraternity; but repudiated that of political equality, by inculcating obedience to Caesar, and to those lawfully in authority. Masonry was the first apostle of Equality. In the Monastery there is fraternity and equality, but no liberty. Masonry added that also, and claimed for man the three-fold heritage, Liberty, Equality, and Fraternity" (Pike, *Morals and Dogma,* p. 23).

This is a good example of syncretism. In fact, it is more. It is the claim of a religion.

Prayer is most important in the lodge. The rites, ceremonies, and meetings always include prayer. Especially is this true during initiation ceremonies of the newly instructed. Hertel's *Bible,* p. 34, says that "In the opening of the lodge, the Great Architect of the Universe must be worshiped, and his blessings upon the work about to be done must be supplicated; at the same time, prayer should be offered for peace and harmony in the closing of the lodge." This non-descriptive "Great Architect" "must be worshiped." Who is he? Any "god" you design. Prayer to a deity is a fundamental dogma of Masonry.

The prayers, however, are not offered in the name of Jesus, despite the Biblical teaching that prayer prayed only in the name of Jesus is valid. The reason Christ is omitted is because of the lodge's attempt to be universal. Mackey in the *Encyclopedia of Freemasonry,* Vol. 1, p. 149, says: "But its universality is its boast. In its language citizens of every nation may converse; at its altars men of all religions may kneel; to its creed disciples of every faith may subscribe." Pike claims that at Masonic "altars the Christian, the Hebrew, the Moslem, the Brahmin, the followers of Confucius and Zoroaster, can assemble as brethren and unite in prayer to the one God. . . . " Jesus said that all men should honor the Son even as they honor the Father.

The attitude of the lodge toward God and the ideas of prayer are quite similar to those of a great number of people in our American society who know nothing of lodge teachings. Many Americans, it seems, are willing to concede validity to any religion, any god to which a person may submit. A similar attitude is found in Masonry, as stated in the *Short Talk Bulletin,* Vol. 36, No. 8, p. 7. "The chaplain of the masonic lodge who prays as the voice of the lodge does not pray in the name of the Carpenter of Nazareth or the name of Jehovah or the name of Allah. He prays to the Grand Artificer or the Great Architect of the Universe. Under that title men of all faiths may find each his own deity. Failure to mention any deity by name is not denial, but merely the practice of a gracious courtesy, so that each man for whom prayer is offered can hear the name of his own deity in the all inclusive title of Great Architect."

Evaluate these examples of prayer: "O Lord, we beseech Thee to bless the work of our Order. May the lessons we here teach be the means of making us better in Thy sight. May we practice in our daily lives the trustful faith of Job so that our reward will be showered upon us. Amen" (from the Ritual of the Order of Job's Daughters). "Go with this sister every step of this initiation, show her that we teach Thy truth, not only for this moment, but for life eternal. Amen" (prayer to define the purpose prayed before the White Altar of Holy Promise of the Order of Rainbow).

Jesus said that to deny Him before men would bring denial of us before His Father in heaven.

It is interesting to note that only in the 18th and 30th degrees of Scottish Rite Masonry and in the Knights Templar Degree of the York Rite Masonry is it permissible to use the name of Jesus Christ in prayer. This privilege is given in respect to those who follow the Christian religion and its teaching. It is a concession granted to those bothered by the Christless prayers prayed in the Blue Lodge.

People, including some Christians, have a strange view of prayer. They feel prayer is the key which unlocks the door to God's house. They think that when they fold their hands and bow their heads, this is how they rap on God's door. Some even think that "Dear God" or "Dear Father in heaven" are attention getters. Jesus, in the Sermon on the Mount, told us that, *before* we ask, the Father knows our needs.

What is the moving power of our prayers? Is it not the Holy Spirit who lives in us, that is, in our bodies, which are His temples? If that is so, and it is, and if it is the Triune God to whom we pray, and it is, then what is prayer? Prayer is God talking to Himself through you. Prayer is not so much the activity of the individual as it is the activity of God, who lives in him. Prayer is God putting the individual on His frequency. Prayer, as communication, can only come when God creates the faith in the heart of the person praying—praying always in "Jesus' name." The ability to communicate with God is the result of the grace extended by God, proof of the restoration of the lost image of Adam. Prayer pre-supposes the relationship of the individual with the Father, created by the reconciling, redemptive action of Jesus Christ, our Lord. This is not what the lodge teaches.

Every Christian needs the conviction of the girl who was asked to pray a public prayer at which many non-Christians would be present. The daughter of a Baptist minister, she wrote her prayer and ended it with the phrase "in Jesus name." Showing her prayer to the vice-principal of the school, he suggested that "we wanted a non-denominational prayer that would satisfy everyone. After all, we expect to have some Jewish people attending the function, so I suggest ending the prayer with something like, 'in God's name.' We all pray to the same God." The girl responded by saying, "If I can't say what I believe, I won't say anything at all."

Another disturbing practice of the lodge is the emphasis it places on giving aid and defense to a fellow Mason, even if he is guilty of a crime, except in the case of murder and treason. Some versions of the oath used by the Royal Arch require the candidate to swear that "I will assist a Companion Royal Arch Mason when I see him engaged in any difficulty, and will espouse his cause so far as to extricate him from the same, whether he be right or wrong." Murder and treason are not excepted as in the Blue Lodge. That is to say, a Royal Arch Mason is sworn to help another even though he is guilty of murder or treason. Can you imagine a defendant, lawyer, judge, and member of a jury all being Royal Arch Masons bringing justice to bear in a case?

Because of the fraternity emphasized in the lodge, favoritism is often practiced in employment, letting of contracts, business deals, and other functions in society. Likewise, when someone has left the lodge, recriminations are sometimes taken if possible with that person's job, station in life, position in a company, etc. There is even evidence of job recriminations taken against workers who have been members of The Lutheran Church—Missouri Synod simply because of its witness that the lodge is an un-Christian cult, even though such workers were never members of the lodge.

6

Some Doctrinal Comparisons

The Christian should have great concern about preserving his Biblical heritage. Jesus said that if we loved Him we would keep His commandments. St. Paul warned Timothy about people who would try to remove from Christianity the Truth which he preached, a warning he strongly gave during his final imprisonment in Rome. It was a warning he also gave to the pastors of Asia Minor at his tear-filled Miletus farewell. St. John repeatedly warned his "little children" about those who would corrupt the teachings of the Redeemer. Jesus warned His followers to remember His words. Through Moses, God told the Israelites to make every home a school with the parents responsible for continually telling their children about their heritage as God's chosen people and the great acts performed in their behalf by a gracious God. Joshua, too, at the settlement of the Promised Land, warned the people never to forsake the Lord's ways. The Bible is full of admonishment and warning not to let the teachings of Scripture be lost.

It is in this same spirit that these pages are written. They come as a warning. Our neglect, ignorance, or rejection of evaluating what the lodge cult says and does is to invite its influence upon our lives. Even as "eternal vigilance" is the price we Americans must pay in order to keep our freedoms from being removed, so also is it with our spiritual heritage. Therefore, we would like to *review* some of the major differences between lodgery and Christianity. The purpose is to show that lodgery conflicts with Christianity. Hopefully this will cause the reader to give a loving witness to others about these contradictions.

The differences which are outlined here will deal with God, man, immortality of the soul, the Bible, prayer, and secrecy.

The first and most glaring contradiction between the lodge and Christianity centers on God. Although the lodge demands belief in a "Supreme Being," although it uses the terms "god," "Lord," The All-Seeing Eye," etc., and although they form a theology about their "god" as to what he does, the lodge very carefully refuses to confess the God of the Scriptures. A definition of the Person of God is avoided. There is no identification of the Father, Son, and Holy Spirit in the lodge, nor any phrase which would identify God as the Trinity. The lodge simply by omission denies the revealed God of the Bible. This offends the Christian—or it should! The Christian is taught from the Bible that there is no salvation, no god other than the Lord of Lords, the Holy Trinity, and that to be saved it is essential to believe and confess this God.

Jesus is the "Word made flesh." He is the great "Light" the Masonic order tries to discover in its search for the Truth but never finds. "Whoever has seen Me has seen the Father," Jesus said.

So strongly do the Masons regard a belief in a "Supreme Being" that they ousted an entire atheistic congregation from their premises. An atheistic Rabbi and his 140 member congregation in Birmingham, Mich., were refused further use of the Masonic Temple in early 1965. The St. Louis

Post-Dispatch, on March 21, 1965, said that "theological reasons" were given as the reason for the decision. The Masons insisted that a positive commitment to the existence of some kind of supreme being was required for use of their temple.

"FREEMASONRY—A SIMPLE RELIGIOUS FAITH" is the title of an article on the cover of the *Royal Arch Mason,* a monthly periodical, Vol. V, No. 9, March 1957, which says, "We have but one dogma, a belief in God, but this is so firmly established as the principal foundation-stone of the brotherhood that no one can ever be admitted a member of an English-speaking lodge without a full and free acceptance thereof. In all reference to the Deity, God is reverently spoken of as the Great Architect of the Universe. . . . Upon this foundationstone we construct a simple religious faith—the Fatherhood of God, the Brotherhood of Man, and the Immorality of the Soul—simple, but all-efficient. By reason of this simple creed, Freemasonry has been able to attract and accept as members of the Fraternity adherents of every religious faith in the world—Christians, Jews, Hindoos, Mohammendans, Pharisees, Buddhists, and others—atheists alone being excluded."

In the experience of this writer most Christians who are members of the lodge do not share our concern over the Masonic compromise of God, nor agree that they are worshiping an idol at the lodge. And this is the difficulty. They say that although they use the term "Supreme Architect of the Universe" they understand him to be their Triune God—especially in a lodge made up mostly of Christians. To them it is just another descriptive name for God, and they see nothing wrong about it—even though the Bible never limits God to these terms.

It is our claim that to avoid the revealed Scriptural names for God is a deliberate attempt to deceive by reducing Christianity to just another of the religions of the world. What is even worse, it is succeeding. By doing this, the lodge effectively de-emphasizes the Person and work of Jesus Christ.

And this brings us to the second conflict existing between the lodge and Christianity—that of man. Masonry teaches that man has a "rough and imperfect nature," but this is as close as they come to saying that man is originally sinful. The reason, most probably, is that if Masonry teaches the Scriptural truth of man's sinful nature, then they would also have to teach salvation by some means. The lodge would then have to deal with Jesus, the Redeemer. Rather, the lodge simply accepts the idea of salvation as something which will happen to all who live a morally upright life. It makes no attempt to identifying what is rejection of God's truth. It does say that good works are necessary for admission into the "Grand Lodge above where the Supreme Grand Master presides." Every Mason in "good standing" is said to be in that glorious number because he was faithful in practicing the principles of the Craft while here on earth. The Lodge makes no attempt to exclude any person from "going to his just reward," but it does guarantee every faithful Mason membership in that "Grand Lodge above." And it does so without any reference to Jesus, His death and resurrection, man's repentance, God's grace, and the like. Therefore, we conclude the lodge is a religion—a Christless religion—and thus a cult, a cult totally incompatible with Christianity and to be avoided by every Christian.

Immortality of the soul is the third major conflict between lodgery and Christianity. Some of what was said in the above paragraphs would apply here, so we will not repeat. We will add just a few lines to what has been said. Immortality is a lodge teaching which had been adopted from Christianity. But that is all that has been adopted—the simple teaching of immortality. The lodge has eliminated the truth that eternal life in heaven is purely a gift of God, that Jesus by His death and resurrection has reconciled sinful man to God, that the Holy Spirit brings men to believe and have faith in Christ as their personal Savior from all sin. Or to say it differently, the lodge is immortality, with or without Christ.

Another conflict deals with what role the Bible plays in the life of the lodge. It is considered a "Sacred Volume," but just one of the many such books of the world. The "Sacred Volume" is one of the three indispensable "tools" of the lodge temple. It does not always mean the Holy Bible. It may be found that in the majority of local lodges in America the Holy Bible is open on the lodge altar, but this is because the religion of the majority of members determines what "Sacred Volume" is used in that particular lodge.

The display of the "Sacred Volume" does not mean that it is used. Just as a family Bible displayed in a home in some prominent place does not mean that it is opened and used, neither does an open Bible on the lodge altar mean that it is used. We do know that lodgery has an already developed educational system. Lodgery does not accept the Holy Bible as the only inspired, infallible, inerrant Word of God. It cannot. This would be unacceptable to all lodge members who were not Christian.

Stil another conflict is prayer. From the moment of ones arrival in the Entered Apprentice Degree, prayer is enjoined on the lodge member. Now it does not offend us that there is prayer. What we wonder is, first, to whom is the prayer addressed? Next, with whom is the prayer shared? Then, is it prayed "in Jesus name"? Also, is confession of sins and the acceptance of the forgiveness of Christ a part of the prayer life?

These questions are rhetorical—the answers are obvious. We Christians, praying in the name of Jesus, always address the Father, Son, and Holy Spirit. Our prayer life is very personal because it reaches to the depths of our souls. We share it cautiously and selectively. When someone else prays with us, speaking the words in our behalf, we have given them permission to talk to God for us. It is neither safe nor right to permit others to lead us in prayer unless we trust their beliefs. It follows, then, that for us it is unthinkable for a Christian Mason to permit a Jewish Worshipful Master or a Unitarian Masonic Chaplain to lead him in prayer. This is so obvious that we wonder how any Christian can accept such a situation.

Finally, we call attention to the secrecy of the lodge, and not because we think it is a major offense or that we are jealous of Masonic secrets. Most lodges, including the Masonic, have been demonstrably unsuccessful in maintaining secrecy. Rather, our concern comes because of the effects secrecy has upon the individual Mason who is in discussion with his pastor or wife. On many occasions this writer has talked with a Mason about Masonry. For the most part it is a monologue. At a certain point in the conversation the Mason simply "clams up." He refuses to talk anymore. There is much he tries to hide because he has been sworn to secrecy.

Usually the relationship he built with the pastor deteriorates from this point onward. Even if the pastor succeeds in convincing him that the lodge should be avoided, that lodge teachings are in conflict with Christianity, the Mason quietly recalls the fraternal relations with other Masons or family influences so that he would not usually withdraw his membership even if he were to admit that the pastor is right.

If what the lodge has to offer is as spiritually beneficial as Masonry says it is, then why is it so necessary to keep it secret? If something is so righteous, so admirable, so important that it even gets you into heaven, they why the veil? One would think it would be wise to open up the lodge doors for the world to look in. Instead, the doors are open only to those who take the oath of secrecy even before they know what it is they must keep secret. In other words, the candidate for the Masonic degrees is required to take the oath before he is told what it is that must be always concealed and never revealed. To take an oath merely "as a form you go through" is dishonesty toward the lodge itself. Lodge members have every right to expect more of a Christian than that he will seek his Lord's endorsement merely as a matter of convenience. Robert Bolt, in his introduction to his play, *A Man for All Seasons,* speaks of an oath on the part of a Christin as

> an invitation to God, an invitation God would not refuse, to act as a witness and to judge. . . . A man takes an oath only when he wants to commit himself quite exceptionally to the statement, when he wants to make an identity between the truth of it and his own virtue; he offers himself as a guarantee.

As Christians we need to be reminded of the seriousness of oathtaking and with whom the oath is taken. Please refer to 1 Cor. 3:16-17; 6:19-20.

7

What We Can Learn from the Lodge

There are many good things about lodgery to which your attention is now called.

First, fraternalism. Americans are joiners. No matter what interests a person may have, someone, somewhere has organized the right organization for him. This is because we Americans want to be a part of people and movements. The lodge provides a close-knit group of people with similar backgrounds and interests. It works hard to build a feeling of brotherhood among its members. True concern for each other is often expressed in a variety of ways, such as defending each other, aiding each other in all ways, caring for families and the aged of fellow Masons, and knowing that all members of the lodge will come to your support.

Loyalty is another admirable quality of the lodge. Seldom, if ever, do you hear a lodge member "bad mouth" his organization, his leaders, or his fellow members. They really stick together, and any differences they may have are handled discreetly. We Christians could learn much here. We not only find reason to "knock" our pastor and fellow members, but our entire church body—and openly, too, as in the public press. Our troubles too could be handled more discreetly.

Patriotism is another admirable quality of the lodge. We are living in an era in American history that tends to look at patriotism as support of "the establishment." Lodges always endeavor to instill patriotism in their members, considering it a part of their total purpose. We admire them for their emphasis, and urge them to increase their efforts.

Moral teachings can also be praised within the lodge. With the sinking of public morality, we must admire anyone who will still teach and inculcate a morally upright life. If the lodge wants to use symbolic tools to teach their morals, we have no objection. In fact, the only objection we have with their teaching of morals is that they claim that by these morals they earn eternal life—which is work righteousness. The teaching of morals, as such, is good.

We would also like to praise the lodge for its humanitarianism. Hospitals, homes for aged, circuses, post-season charity football games, and the like are magnificent gestures of human compassion. We thank God for these works and acts of charity, knowing all along that we Christian churches could be doing so much more than we are.

8

How to Witness to the Lodge

There are many ex-lodge members in our Lutheran Church—Missouri Synod, as there are in other denominations. People do leave the lodge. In most cases, however, it is difficult to convince a member to disassociate from the lodge.

The best way to witness about the lodge is to teach our children and adults what causes our concern before they get involved. Synod-wide instruction on Fraternalism has appeared at regular intervals in our official periodicals beginning as early as 1849. This present series of booklets by our Board for Evangelism, in response to a resolution adopted by the Anaheim Convention in 1975, is a continuation of our witness.

Witnessing directly to a lodge member is most difficult. Not only is there the secrecy barrier discussed in the previous chapter hindering any real progress, but many Christians have joined the lodge without knowing of the contradictions between lodgery and Christianity. Some were unable to recognize these contradictions as they were instructed in the lodge because they know little of Christianity. There are at least three reasons making it most difficult to witness to and win a lodge member.

First, the deception of the person was skillfully performed. The philosophy symbolized, for example, by the Lambskin Apron is so simple and pure to the ears and eyes. Second, after taking the oath, paying the dues, and enjoying the fraternal atmosphere, the person will hardly admit to his error. To admit it will take repentance and humility—and human nature is not inclined toward either. Third, pressure applied by the lodge brothers is often intense. The consequences of leaving the lodge may have life-long significance.

Many lodge members contend that their lodge in no way interferes with their church life—in fact, they say, it helps them. When a lodge member thinks this, it usually means that he refuses to admit there is a conflict in the teachings of the lodge and Christianity. It usually means that the door is closed for further consideration.

The worst possible way for a person to witness to a lodge member is to make statements that are not true about what the lodge is or does. Another ineffective witness is to simply say, "Well, my church says it is wrong to join the lodge." Still another ineffective witness is to argue to the point of anger.

Knowledge about what the lodge teaches and practices is most important in witnessing to a lodge member, or to one considering lodge membership. Knowing what the actual conflicts are between lodgery and Christianity will arm the person with confidence, the certainty so necessary to counteract the feeling of insecurity when the discussion becomes heated. More important is this: a person knows—really knows— then he can ask penetrating and thought producing questions as his method of making his point. It is not too difficult to catch the lodge member in his own contradictions if the right questions are asked.

An example of how the question approach can work is this:

Question: It is my understanding that the lodge prides itself in its educational program.

Answer: Yes, we do require our members to know a few things.

Question: Would you share a little with me?

(At this point the lodge member is on the defensive, giving thought to just how much he can say.)

Answer: Well, I can't tell you much, but if you care to join you would learn it all.

Question: Is what you learn in the lodge important to you?

Answer: Yes.

Question: Well, then, it should be important to me also? Why must I join first in order to learn something that will help me? Why shouldn't everyone be told?

(It is not important to carry this discussion any further because the point has already been made. Move on to another subject, but still use the question method.)

Question: Is the lodge a religion to you?

Answer: Absolutely not!

Question: Do you pray in the lodge?

Answer: Yes, but it's only to open our meetings.

Question: Do you pray to God?

Answer: Of course we do.

Question: Who does the lodge say is God?

Answer: We don't tell any member who God is, each person is free to think of God as he wants.

Question: Is this what the Bible teaches?

Answer: Not all members believe the way Christians do.

Question: If you were leading the lodge in prayer, would you use the name of the Triune God, ending it with "This we pray in Jesus name"?

Answer: Well, we use the prayers printed in our book.

(Now the person realizes that someone else has pre-determined what the prayers would be, that the Bible is rejected by some "lodge brothers"— which has to leave a crack in the fraternal relationship, that avoidance of the Triune God is really a denial of Him.)

This is enough to give the reader an idea of both the style and content of the question approach. It needs to be emphasized that the questions need to be asked without sarcasm, in complete humility and understanding, yet firmly headed toward the goal of demonstrating the conflict existing between lodgery and Christianity. The important thing to remember is that unless the lodge member is convinced in his own heart that he is wrong he is still going to retain the same opinion.

The ultimate goal—that of changing a lodge member to a former lodge member—is achieved only by the working of the Holy Spirit through our words. We are dependent upon the Holy Spirit to change people's heart. He does this when we use words which point to our sins and our forgiveness in Jesus. Nowhere else will people hear of the Good News of salvation or the redeeming work of Christ other than from a Christian source. Even if the lodge member claims to be a Christian, he needs to hear the message of salvation from us. Simple words about the cross of Jesus are the most important words anyone could hear, professing Christians included!

The absence of a Christ-confessing fraternal association will be evident to the lodge member if we simply keep emphasizing the love Jesus has for all of us. Acceptance is what we need and look forward to receiving from another. Jesus loves us, even when we are bad. We, too, need to love one another, even when we are bad. If we do, the friendship will be long lasting and genuine. This is what will deeply impress a lodge member about us, and others as well.

Careful thought and planning needs to precede our witness to a lodge member if at all possible, taking the matter to the Lord in prayer. We should be specific in such prayers, remembering the person by name and asking the Lord to take some specific action with respect to his lodge membership.

Reading material, but not too much of it, should be left with the lodge member upon completion of our visits. We would like to think that this booklet would be good for this purpose. If our conversation has been delivered with understanding, humility, and patience, the person will read what we leave with him. Otherwise it will be discarded quickly as though he were trying to get rid of you, and the conflict, as soon as possible.

Conclusion

The Lutheran Church—Missouri Synod has always regarded false teachings and practices to be destructive of the freedom the Gospel gives to us. Falsehoods are shackles which chain men to the darkness of unbelief. In order that our members may not give away the freedom earned for us by Jesus, we ask that no member join an organization which destroys the Christ-centered, Biblical-orientated church which is our heritage. The objections a Christian has with regard to certain organizations could be summarized as follows:

1. They claim to offer moral and spiritual enlightenment which is not available in Holy Scripture.
2. They teach that all religions, in reality, worship the same God, but under different names.
3. They declare that all men have equal access to God, their attitude toward Jesus Christ being unimportant.
4. They teach that eternal life is the reward which God gives for virtuous living.

May you, and all members of our church, always be READY TO GIVE AN ANSWER TO THE LODGE.

Bibliography

Acker, Julius W., *Strange Altars*. St. Louis: Concordia Publishing House, 1965.

Hannah, Walton, *Christian By Degrees*. London: Britons Publishing Company, 1964.

Hannah, Walton, *Darkness Visible*. London: Britons Publishing Company, 1963.

Lochhaas, Philip, Various releases on specific lodges published by the Commission on Organizations of The Lutheran Church—Missouri Synod, 500 N. Broadway, St. Louis, Mo. (offset printed).

Vindex (pen name), *Light Invisible*. London: Britons Publishing Company, 1964.

Whalen, William J., *Christianity and American Freemasonry*. Milwaukee: The Bruce Publishing Company, 1958.